THE BLAZING FURNACE

AN ECLECTIC COLLECTION OF EXPERIMENTAL POEMS WITH IMAGES

ROBERT MADDOX-HARLE

Cyberwit.net
HIG 45 Kaushambi Kunj, Kalindipuram
Allahabad - 211011 (U.P.) India
http://www.cyberwit.net
Tel: +(91) 9415091004
E-mail: info@cyberwit.net

Printed at VCORRE PRESS.

"This is what haunts [re poetry]
a world where magic is possible,
where chance reigns, where
metaphors have their supreme
logic, where imagination is free
and truthful."
Charles Simic, 1985

Preface

This is my fourth volume of poetry. The first, *Scratches & Deeper Wounds* (1996); second, *Mechanisms of Desire* (2012); third, *Winds of Infinity* (2016). As the subtitle says, it is an eclectic collection of experimental poems. Poetry seems to be gaining an increase in popularity in recent years, very encouraging, perhaps because of the global internet influence. Much of this work is simply rehashing existing styles and subject matter, these have their place in society of course, however, we need to move forward with literature and experiment with new forms and challenge the status quo, not necessarily in an aggressive, destructive or political way which was characteristic of some avant-garde and neo-avant-garde movements, but in experimental and unique ways.

I have tried to do this with most of the poems in this collection, a few are fairly traditional but most attempt to offer a new, perhaps challenging approach to poetry relevant to the 21st century. As I have mentioned previously, postmodernism has attempted to destroy the sublime and numinous. The new art and poetics in this post postmodern era must help *restore our abandoned metaphysical and spiritual modes of being*. This art also now in the postdigital age must re-humanise the technology of the digital. We need to embrace sustainability, and re-envisage the *"mysterium, tremendum et fascinans."*

My connection with India over the past ten years has been quite extraordinary, dare I say a karmic connection. The way Indian poets, scholars and publishers have embraced my work and offered support, not the least of which is the offer to publish my books, is something that has never happened in Australia.

I would especially like to thank Karunesh Agrawal (cyberwit) and Sudarshan Kcherry (Authorspress). There are too many others to mention individually but I must thank,
Sunil Sharma, Jaydeep Sarangi and K.V. Dominic for their support, and selecting me for the *Lifetime Achievement Award 2021*, (GIEWEC) (For his continued dedication and promotion for Indian Writing in English).

Robert Maddox-Harle, Australia, 2022
robert @maddoxharle.com

Contents

Sand Dunes At Dusk

the sand dunes - still warm
surround me as the sun departs,
each rippling ridge receding
receding,   receding,   receding
disappearing in the salty saffron haze.

relentlessly the waves crash,
then swirl and whoosh towards me
swirling-whooshing, swirling-whooshing, swirling-whooshing,
crash-swirl-whoosh, crash-swirl-whoosh, crash-swirl-whoosh.

incessant screeching of gleaming white gulls
competing with the waves crashing-swirling-whooshing
create a counterpoint cacophony
ever rising, surging, silvering
screeching, swirling, crashing, receding.
then the crashing, whooshing, swirling starts again
crash-swirl-whoosh, crash-swirl-whoosh, crash-swirl-whoosh.

a mysterious moon, rising ever so slowly
slowly,   slowly,   slowly
rising slowly,   rising slowly,   rising slowly
casts silvery shadows
dancing fluorescent, iridescent, hauntingly
dancing on the silvery, swirling, crashing
Crashing - Crashing - Crashing
the crashing haunts me, haunts me, haunts me
as the darkness descends
and steals my eyes away.

This poem was inspired by Philip Glass's "Glassworks" composition.

Nothing Can Be Done

In the swirling, turning world
things - are as they are,
the only time, "here – now",
the only vision is infinity,
an endless mirror of expectation
emanating from the Music of the Spheres,
filled with the wisdom of "no-thing".

Play On Harry!

Here rests the enlightened heart
beating time in endless harmony
amidst the turning and swirling,
in this transient glimpse of absurdity.

"For everything there is a time"
a time when things can be done,
a time for reflection and recollection,
a time when - Nothing Can Be Done.

Screeching Blackness

an insect shrills the night air
shrill … shrill ………………………… SHRILL!
all becomes silent and then ……………….. CRASH!
echoes crash the forest dark ….. CRASH!
screaming blackness bounces off old trees
a machine hummms in the distance …… WAITING!
an insect-like machine hummming ….SCREAMING,
waiting for its master ……………….. WAITING!
Kafka is hiding in the shadows,
more insects scream and screech and shrill,
screech – scream - shrill
silence blankets the darkness – quiet – quiet – quiet
a heartbeat of silence then ……….. SCREECH!
the dark noise is menacing, penetrating
violent ….. CRASH!
echoes crash the forest dark ……… CRASH!
Murderous-like screams ……. screaming,
unforgiving ….. brutal ….. intense
TWANG! ……………….. push-pull ……………..TWANG!
ping ….. ping ….. TWANG!
high pitch vibrations …… violently agitated
shake the leaves from trees,
they fall forever into blackness
as the forest falls silent.

This poem was inspired by the work of composer Karlheinz Stockhausen,
especially his work "Kontakte"

"Dark Forest" (photo Robert Maddox-Harle)

Nasturtiums

Carefree times long past
the joy of birdsong waking
"Listen to the Magpies singing"
Grandma taught me to cherish the wonder.

Nasturtiums in our new garden
time-travel back to Grandma's,
realisation of things lost
scents of mouldy cupboards reinforce the regression,
the passage of years so cruel.

The loss of spontaneous wonder
not totally gone perhaps
maybe simply tempered by time.
Nasturtiums and magpies are markers
keys to regaining the joys of childhood.

Travelling Light

Mohandas Gandhi travelled light
a loin cloth, a shawl, round glasses
his meagre trademark,
favouring the freedom of the Everyman
over the encumbrances of wealth and power,
he lit a blazing candle
so all the world could see,
could see the path to freedom.

Defying the overlords of authority
the power brokers of control,
through nonviolent civil resistance
he lit a light eternal,
dissipating the curse of colonialism
the superiority of British rule,
diluting insidious religious contamination.
Fear not great Gandhi
like Nelson Mandela and Martin Luther King Jr.
your imprisonment by the fearful cowards
was not in vain.

Now his **Way** is embraced by the Everyman,
saving our forests and the earth herself,
saving the poor from ruthless domination,
empowering the powerless.
A **Way** with dignity and with no ….. blood ….. shed

Mahatma Gandhi – the venerable one – great soul
your own blood was **not** shed in vain.

Red Queen

The Red Queen stands aloof
commanding her subjects with shouts,
mysterious in her gaze
compelling in her countenance.

Agitated she invites the Mad Hatter to lunch,
"Bring the red tea and a menu now!"
"What are the ingredients of Rabbit Pie?"
she screeches sourly.

Sugar, water, salt
Salted plums, thickener, tomato paste
Food acids (330, 260), garlic, ginger
Rabbit on the bone
Dripping, flour, flavour enhancer (621)
Caramel (150a)

The tension rises, looks are exchanged.

Exclaiming rudely the Mad Hatter shouts
"I do not eat Rabbit Pie!"
"Then", off with your hat!
and then, off with your head!"

Remember what the Dormouse said?
"Feed   your   head".

"The Axe" (Time release photo Sandra Joran)

greed

greed .. greed

greed .. greed .. greed

greed .. greed.. greed .. greed

greed .. greed.. greed .. greed .. greed

greed .. greed.. greed .. greed .. greed

greed .. greed.. greed .. greed

greed .. greed.. greed

greed .. greed

greed

Seeking the Butterfly Nebula

Searching for the illusive entrance
distorted pixels dance in my face,
invisible time-warp portals close
then open to reveal new worlds,
direct dynamic neural labyrinths
editing complex interconnections
harness the energy of data molecules,
they hint at the universal truth
a truth beyond all repressive doctrines,
sweeping laser-like beams
bluish, hypnotise me
entangle me
my heart races erratically,
another unchartered time-warp portal opens
a three dimensional Yantra
draws me forward seductively,
I merge with the Zero-point-field.

No longer slowed by space-time constraints
everything is becoming possible,
I ponder 4,000 light years to the Butterfly Nebula
186,000x60x60x24x365x4000 – the old way,
before I can finish the mental arithmetic
the Butterfly Nebula is coming into view,
vibrant colours, swirling, intertwining
dancing in unison before my eyes
carried through a labyrinth of colour
I emerge glowing
heading towards the centre of Infinity.
Pondering the Magical Blue Knight
he miraculously appears,
we speed towards his homeland
a sapphire blue crystal geodesic planet.

Fondly I remember Tibet my own homeland,
I am floating up long stone steps
carrying me to the Potala Palace
a sanctuary on the roof of the Earth world,
I seek the Golden Yantra – a portal to transformation.

Shrouded Coffin

The intrapsychic coffin is shrouded
a sickly white-grey mist obscures its plaque,
the coffin's presence a mystery,
it suddenly materialising remains unanswered.

Throwing the Tarot yields The Moon,
four golden Yods fall from her body
two towers are the gateway to Resurrection
the dark flux of night dominates ….
this coffin is deceptive,
search past the falsity of the obvious
is the wisdom of this Luna card.

The mist lifts and reveals an inscribed plaque
"Within this tomb lies the answer,
the answer to the illusion of space-time reality",
to open the coffin an esoteric key is needed ….
a ventriloquist's phantom chant
echoing an incantation harmoniously,
an incantation from the heart of the Golden Yantra.

The chanting slows and softens
the dark flux of night
is drawn apart by slivers of moonlight,
in the yellow gloom the coffin lid opens,
an effigy of Salvador Dali grins,
a golden clock balances on his chest
the time …. one minute to midnight.

"Danger Death" (Original photo Carl Heydon)

Closing The Circle

So I return to constant searching
beyond subatomic particles
beyond the swirling dance of matter,
Inner space defines the search parameters,
the structure remains illusive
archetypes and symbols taunt us.
Pure Divine Water - the symbol of fundamental matter
Mother is Matter - this archetype of Mother-Matter
encompassing - sustaining - is the Prima Materia.

Waves in flux give rise to particles
What influences the wave to Become,
to become a standing wave
then to become a particle?

Cosmic inflation
unification of inner and outer space
closing in a full circle.
only mysticism can know the arcane truth
the Euroboros symbol – ancient, ubiquitous
explains the "closing of the circle",
Alchemists the keepers of this shrouded secret,
their Blazing Furnace manifests - The Stone.
The Stone – key to the origin of the structure,
the genesis of the Cosmos.

The Great Work creates this sacred object,
its harmonic resonance the connection to the Source,
the key to:
transfiguration, transubstantiation, transformation.
Everything becomes possible:
access to all knowledge
ability to transcend the illusory shackles of space-time

able to function non-locally and acausally
to become ONE with The Source.

Sea Ghosts

False hopes, empty promises
the screams resonate inside her paintings
weathered by a surgeon's scalpel,
those penetrating eyes perched atop a scythe
drag her bewildered mind back to her head,
the deceptive spirit of mortality
is a discordant dirge,
twisted strings entangle web-like
as the cracks beneath the White lies explode.

A butcher bird descends, perching lightly
the arms of anguish pulsate
as exotic distant voices echo,
an owl screeches in the brightness
spirits of the slaughtered indigenous chill her eyelids,
the screeching,
the death-cries of the sea ghosts
howl in deep blackness across the rocky foreshore.

On The Road

Onward ever onward into Forever >>>>>>>>>>>>
over Long Hollow Creek
over *Clay Pothole Creek*
terrifying trembling trucks thunder past
Onward ever onward into Forever >>>>>>>>>>>>
over *Poison Swamp Creek*
Onward towards a vile insidious poison
over *Tommy Swamp*
Now in the land of the Neanderthal Nationals.

On the right – extreme - the *Harvest Bible Church*
a sickening Billboard assaults my face
Further into *Calibre Country*
Ammo – Firearms – Shooting
another sickening Billboard assaults my face
Fishers, Shooters and Farmers Party
another sickening Billboard assaults my face
(Quote: "He didn't even know what hit him!")
(Note: Borsak's comment after he shot a magnificent,
mature elephant for sport with his high power hunting
rifle – such a Brave Man?)
over *Dead Bird Lead Creek*
terrifying trembling trucks thunder past
Onward ever onward into Forever >>>>>>>>>>
over *Black Waterhole Creek.*

zero emissions = zero jobs = zero future
another sickening Billboard assaults my face
over *Splitters Swamp Bridge*
Now in the land of golden grain
millions of acres of monoculture into Forever >>>>>>>>>>
past a dead Roo – stinking bloody pulp
terrifying trembling trucks thunder past
Onward ever onward into Forever >>>>>>>>>>

Towards a Zero Future ……….. Forever >>>>>>>>>>>>>

Footnote:
1 – In Australia one major political party is the National Party.
*2 – Another very minor party is the Fishers, Shooters and Farmers Party –
Robert Borsak is a leading gun in this party.*
*3 – Harvest Church is an extreme right-wing orientated Christian church
which is Pentecostal.*
4 – All creek names are real.

Fractal Dimensions

The evolving pollution of thought
always buzzing
assaults my senses,
and gravity exerts its compelling crush.

Supermarket abundance beckons
taking on traits of fractal dimensions,
there is a liminal zone here!
Does it have a contact number?
Does it have a URL?
How should I know, always sleeping under bark bits
deep in a forest of stupidity
where the dominant order is C – C – G – Em.

2 cups of flour;
1 cup of sugar,
1 teaspoon of nutmeg;
500 grams butter
1 cup of champagne;
Cook for as long as it takes.

Lying awake sometimes,
drifting with the melodies of spiders weaving,
Click, Click – shuttle through
Click, Click – shuttle through,
the web is a sticky satin silver
a shroud for unwary sycophants.

"Foggy, then mostly sunny:
Chance of showers:
Little chance of snow:
Top of 18 degrees:
Erosion from hazardous surf conditions:"

The coastal high-rise-horrors precarious,
falling, toppling into the voluptuous surf,
Better call 000!
then write Emergency Poetry!

It started all too early
the lies, deceptions and falsities
peddled with authority and guile
inducing fear and blind obedience
until conformity was assured.

I have been lied to all my life!

Santa Claus brought gifts of gentle deception
down chimneys for fruit-cake and beer,
"Be good or your stocking will be empty"
I was good, the gifts arrived, the beer was gone,
Ho! Ho!

To Church, and then to Sunday School,
Jesus!!
preposterous patriarchal lies
peddled by paedophiles and cunning imbeciles
designed to frighten and control,
Control - Control - Control
Hell-fire and brimstone for eternity
the promised outcome for transgression.

Yes, I have transgressed a thousand times or more!

Falsities at school ended in disaster
wrong subjects, wrong advice, wrong decisions
"No university for you, sorry!"
Liar!
Try the TAFE College young man
more misleading lies, more deceptions,
faith in the "Establishment" dwindled fast.

Then old enough to vote
diligently I analysed the political messages
Ha, these Men were consummate liars
promises, rebuttals, blatant destructive lies
then came Conscription and the lies about a war
a war - Vietnam - a giant incongruous lie.

Then employers lied like politicians
priests still peddled lies
scientists, with hidden agendas lied
they lied about Thalidomide
they lied about Soy
they lied about The Pill
Big pharma lied about ulcers
and my mother died,
doctors deceived about the "cancer cure"
and my brother died.

Time is no longer on my side
the hour glass is out of balance,
cynicism has replaced gullibility
and now I am angry,

STOP TELLING ME LIES!

Stockhausen's Revenge

CRASH!
soft shrills / echo / reverb
reverb / reverb / reverb
industrial / techno / whistle
shrill and brutal
QUITE!
bang / crash
build to crash / shrill whistle
FADE!
soft distant build / fade
build / fade
crash / violent / menacing
frightening old house eerie
mechanical insects
incessant, eating the night
then quiet
fade to black.

Cut Short

it started at five in the morning
falling out of bed,
a strange reaching-out dream
over balanced, flat on my back
the floor was hard and unforgiving.

consult the oracle
Astro-girl in the local tabloid,
You'll have a hard day!
Be careful meeting strangers!
Perhaps a trip down memory lane!

filtering through a box of old cards,
 a get well card from Bhakto
now he's dead
i miss his Zen sayings.
a Christmas card from Derek
now he's dead
i miss his smile and sculptures.
a cartoon card from KAF
now he's dead
i miss Kevin's clay and artistic way.

Another card another one dead
more cards more dead
too many friends, too many family
All dead!

forlorn i threw the cards
one by one into the fire,
the funeral pyre with saddened flames
smoked and roared
as i reflected on these truncated lives.

like young shrubs, tender saplings
mercilessly pulled from the ground
purged before their peak,
All dead!
Dead! Dead! Dead!
the cast became too long to continue,
the sadness too great to swallow!

"Head Stones – Lismore" (photo Robert Maddox-Harle)

The Hospital

An eyelash clears a cinder trapped beneath its rim,
the chained slave is a never ending burden
in different shades of bruised blackness,
then consumable luxuries send intimate messages
extremely crass,
56432-1
so the goose kills the loquacious and inaccessible whores
and everlasting vows are abandoned.

La Saltpetrière – Explosive!
gunpowder blasts transmute to deranged screams
Enter Edvard Munch!
The plough rejects the earth
shrill birds mocking,
this ultimately floats into infinity
all ignoring an oboe's desolate plea.

Next we find the pawnshop of numeric tourism,
this well-considered defence strategy opens the
technological almanac
raising the hospital's permit
and the hysterics are silenced,
SILENCE .. SILENCE .. SILENCE

The soft-hearted and worn down procurements float
as doubt settles into the abysmal lace,
the best-seller an abomination of retrospective lies
answers as the phone rings abruptly.
Hallo!
47 Boulevard de L'hopital.

A mysterious painting hangs abandoned in the hall
its piety risks exposure

functioning as a mirror for psychosis
all creatures disintegrate before its reactive tendrils.

Go Ask Alice

A mysterious unknowable force
flowing forward then backward
hiding secrets within the liminal zone,
archetypes resonate with the force
emanating from within the photonic maze,
the structure of the electromagnetic zero-point field
giving birth to diachronic fractal attractors,
spontaneous communication,
acausal parallelism,
scale invariant Taoism.
the processes hinted at cryptically,
subtly in the De Lapide Philisophico.

Atomic harmonics vibrating
energising the Yin of the Unconscious
and the Yang of the Conscious.
Did Bohm access the field directly?
Did de Broglie's violin's vibrations
harmoniously sympathetically
open the portal to the zero-point field?
the universal all encompassing ontological force
the Prima Materia.
Unknowable using cold hard logic,
inaccessible using Enlightenment reasoning.

STOP!

Before proceeding to GO
observe the cautions
cautions hinted at over millennia,
consult the Tarot
check the astrological timing
check the planetary alignments,

all in the universe is connected
timing is everything.

THEN!

Go ask a Shaman!
Go ask the Indigenous Elders!
Go ask Alice!

Myth Mongers

The obscenity of mediocrity
cuts across the boredom of melting chocolate,
as delusions of nature's ardent love
contract into an insidious digital invasion,
cool reflections of darkness
strut the moon to space
awareness contracts into frightened frames
in a transformation of whiteness
irreverently as blue cold steel.

Sorrowed leaves fall towards the body
turning angrily into frozen Freudian fragments,
the wall of the dream
prospecting the limitations
confirms the validity of the straight jacket.

The green leaf of minimum focus
tries to obey rules which could not exist,
the catechism fails all credibility
the lies of the liturgy, venomous
separating the skins of despots,
the deceivers myth mongers
who hide behind mantles of passion and deception
their journey one of insecurity and destruction.

Enmeshed with the taste of solipsistic rapture
hysterically we scream for signs
from the uncremated dead rotting with binary toxicity,
veering from lingering toxic visions
ancestral roots are severed by an eclipse
the silhouette of a foreign homeland
guarded by silent sentries controlling cyberspace

Hidden Erotica

self-destructive dangers of contemporary life
fuelled by excessive visual images
drowned in proliferating documents
reinforcing the fragility of identity
made worse by the protectors
the guardians of public morality
who decides what is hidden
what is kept secret and mysterious
deviously to add intrigue and desire?

erotic art held by private reclusive investors
investors - not collectors – investors
silently seeking out hidden masterpieces
coveted in dark dungeons for decades
prolific in the Vatican catacombs
an exclusive cult – No Public Admittance.

vast amounts of money move
silently through obscure accounts
naked spread-sheets dancing
glowing in the insipid moonlight
electronically encrypted
NFTs proliferate nightly
sharpening the edge
the cutting edge of a kill
transcontinental clandestine interactions.

purveyors and keepers of the bodies of flesh
taunting enticing glimpses of power
full of intrigue and adventure
actors who navigate the liminal space
a space for private interactive scenarios
through extension, extraction and exploitation

just who is being exploited?
like Orlan obliterating any references to gender
resonating harmoniously with their subjects
reinforcing the anti-life actions of beauty technology
reinforcing the world of neoliberalist abomination
is it possible to unpack, reject or critically eradicate
dissolve this curse from humanity
rid us of the vitriolic power games
absolutely dedicated to self-interest?

Mystic Fire

In the crucible of the turning world
the alchemist's furnace smoulders,
salt, sulphur and mercury fume
pluming like clouds across an endless sky.
A voice booms:
"View the foundations well that here are layd:
This is the seat that the eternall mind
For universall monarchy designd." (1)

The gold of fools is ever tempting
though this is not the gold the furnace yields,
the 'stone' alone transforms vile greed and hate,
the gold of fools feeds this rapacious gluttony
enslaving all who seek the glitter.

The serpent eats its body whole
clearing ash and dross away
as the Phoenix rises from the mystic fire,
soaring higher, ever higher.

The cycle of eternal mind
spiral-spinning, turning, pulsing
forever rising and descending
draws us inward
to find our place within the flame.

(1) From Hermetick Raptures by Torrescissa (Alchemical Poetry 1575 – 1700
ed. R.M. Schuler. pp. 584)

Sound and Fury

Squaring the measure of silence,
silence prevails,
creating quantum computers in our own image
we fail to fathom the master's mutated words.
"We strut and fret our hour upon the stage
And then are heard no more,
our desires are a tale told by an idiot,
full of sound and fury,
Signifying nothing".
The sound and fury is reaching its pinnacle,
the summit of desire is in view.
Reprogram your desire DNA with solitonic futures,
holographic computers networked to the Galactic Centre,
transmute endogenous laser radiation
using social-media interfaces
brand names of domination,
brand names of damnation,
the summit of desire is in view.
Our rose coloured denial-spectacles are turning blue,
the blurred myopic shades fading,
the paradox of stupidity and brilliance peaking,
reaching its crowning.
The Titanic is sinking again,
stressfully unconcerned - we order a new iphone,
stressfully in denial - we eat mangoes in July,
stressfully unaware - we breed like Drosophila.
The obtuse granularity of our denial
is over-shadowed by our desire for desire,
the dark black-hole of our bio-quantum computer
is a teraptosis worm-hole for neuroscientists
which reveals emptiness.
Squaring the measure of emptiness
emptiness prevails,

Squaring the sound of blackness
blackness prevails,
and so it will when we crash into the summit.

Katrina and Dr Mazzner

(An experimental poem in the form of random diary entries set within a frame narrative.)

Dear Dr Mazzner,   Friday May 8, 1998

i phoned the hospital today to talk to you but your secretary told me you were on holidays for two weeks.

my medication doesn't seem to be working properly. sometimes the voices are screaming. i hope i can hold out 'till you come back.

thought i'd go through my diary to see what's happened over the past few years.

you told me it was a good idea to get my feelings out, remember? "Words on paper can help straighten out your head", you said once. i wonder where you are, enjoying yourself, what's a holiday like?

wishes, katrina

PS: i'm still waiting to hear from the Church about an apology and compensation, remember your secretary wrote THAT letter?

****

<u>Personal Diary</u>   <u>18th March 1996</u>

Today i realised i was still alive
the white-coats took me for a walk,
scents of the earth
early flowers and spring buds smiled,
neatly tended hospital grounds
how much i'd missed - did it matter?
drugged, strapped down, electrocuted
incessant blurred nightmare.
today i realised i was still alive.
the future?
memories, fragments of memories
deep-sleep clearing,
bits of someone's life - mine i guess,
was it a year since i went mad?
birds chirped and danced
darting behind happy hyacinths,
puffy clouds looked down - watching me,
would she fall?
the white-coats chatted at a distance
voices, memories of voices
but: no voices, no voices
Oh wondrous day - calm day.
but i was tired
i sat under a huge velvet fig tree,
my body, i still had a body
imagine that, a body that felt.

outside the hospital walls life was moving
cars in the distance, hummed
imagine that, to drive a car
fast - speeding along.

<u>Personal Diary   26th March 1997</u>

Another year has passed
Clozapine - Valium - benzo haze,
rest,
walks,
talks with doctors,
getting strong day by day.
i help the gardeners sometimes
they don't talk to me much,
i've planted seeds, some grew
bursting into bloom - a miracle.
gardeners seem full of love,
i wonder if someone will ever love me?
many times in the black night, i wonder.
i wonder?
i'm not mad; I'M   NOT   MAD!
Doctor said i only have an illness
....S C H I Z O P H R E N I A....
big words are hard for me,
i wonder, did i ever go to school?
so i'd remember, i copied schizophrenia,
Doctor Mazzner left me in his room one day.
alone.

the green-coats always look at me funny
i don't trust them,
they tell the doctor my thoughts
so they can all plot against me.
trying to get rid of me,
secretly.
days drift into other days,
i'm getting strong.
Father O'Brien's voice has disappeared,
has he gone forever and ever?
Doctor Mazzner chased him away with Clozapine.
i'm leaving the hospital,
a room of one's own, in the city.
imagine, a room of my own.
i'm really scared.

<u>Personal Diary</u>   <u>3rd April 1997</u>

My own room, ooh ah!
the white-coats helped me settle,
they didn't have their white coats on today
they were incognito, undercover!
ha! ha! - we tricked the landlady.
Mrs Streng terrified me,
No parties! No pets! No noise!
her eyes made me feel cold.
i checked and double, treble checked
no hidden microphones,
no hidden cameras,

maybe they can spy on me through the TV,
"Cover it up with a cloth, silly".
Night time crept in my window,
i was alone
I can't remember being ON MY OWN before
fear lay me on the bed frozen.
suddenly light flashed my window,
i jumped and screamed
go away, go away.
another flash, cautiously i approached
i laughed and laughed,
my only window looked over a bus terminus
empty buses,
empty buses here and there
row after row of empty lonely seats
followed the driver into the unknown.
medication,
"Take your medication now",
i must remember to take my medication.

<u>Personal Diary</u>   <u>16th June 1997</u>

i cross days off my calendar
like crossing days off my life.
what is my life?
alone in a tiny room
no one visits,
no one,
no one.

only the white-coats to bring medication.
alone in my tiny room,
no one!
the empty buses tease me
i wonder where they go?
tomorrow i'll follow one.

<u>Personal Diary   17th June 1997</u>

Today i ran after the first empty bus,
ran faster as it disappeared,
around the corner
all sorts of people standing in a line
one by one they moved,
stepping into the blue monster,
i got on too!
i had money
the white-coats gave me some,
Clozapine - Valium - money - food,
"How are you?
"See you next week" - bye.
they hardly ever look at me
i don't trust them.
the bus purred along,
ooh, more passengers,
a man sat next to me
i froze.
"Morning" he said,
opening up a huge newspaper,

i should read newspapers too,
too many words might confuse me.
i should try to be like these people,
yes, i'll try.
"Where are you going?" i asked timidly.
"To work of course".
He didn't look up from his paper,
maybe i should try to work?
"How do i get a job?"
i gazed at the shops speeding past
a sign,
a sign in an office window
WORK VACANCY - Apply within.
i jumped up, squashed the man's paper
and rushed to the front bus door,
stop the bus!
the driver looked at me as though i was mad,
i'm not, Dr Mazzner told me
stop the bus now!
the driver screeched to a halt
everybody laughed,
i ran back up the street towards
the sign.

<u>Personal Diary</u>   <u>24th July 1997</u>

imagine, i've been working for five weeks
i cross the days of my calendar,
work close to my room

cleaning out the dirty, empty buses.
i work each night,
i'm not scared
all the lights are blazing
the empty buses haunt me though
the morning's passengers at home
with family, friends
with boyfriends and girlfriends
i wonder if i'll ever have a friend.
i can't talk to people,
they read my thoughts
hurrying away,
sometimes they laugh loud
sometimes they snigger.
i even bought new clothes
new hairstyle, ooh!
i look just like the passengers.
Dr Mazzner called yesterday
two white-coats followed behind,
i said, "The drugs make me too tired"
He said, "We shouldn't reduce the dose"
i said, "we must"
He said, "I'm worried"
i said, "Don't worry, i'm getting strong"
He said, "OK, just a small reduction"
the white-coats didn't say anything
just smiled,
sneaky suspicious smiles,
smirks.

ENERGY! ENERGY! ENERGY!
the Valium haze is lifting,
each day,
stronger and stronger.
Bang! Bang!
"Evening"
Mr Security Guard likes to frighten me
hits his truncheon on the side of the bus
"Don't sneak up on me!"
i tell him every time,
he roars laughing and marches off.
i find things in the empty buses
traces of lives,
lost property
i keep some things
my only link with people.
i hide them in my room
i found a black wallet today,
framed inside
family photo, some money, driver's licence,
imagine zooming along in a car
passing the slow blue monsters.
a family photo
a lady, two children.
i study the photo
and start to cry loudly
louder and harder

i woke up with the sun burning,
my window glass.
i had to destroy the photo
so i burnt it on the stove ring,
the plastic burnt my fingers
it stuck hot,
i couldn't get it off
i screamed out in pain.
"Everything all right?" growled Mrs Streng.
go away you old busybody
i screamed through my door,
then cried alone,
and cried
and cried.

<u>Personal Diary   9th October 1997</u>

ENERGY! had to use up energy
go for a walk
walk see Dr Mazzner
walk to see Dr Mazzner's hospital
yes yes yes.
when i leave my room
i hide my secret things,
i hide them in the oven.
never use the oven,
never learned to cook
i eat from packets and cans.
passing people fast

shops of people fast
cars and buses full of people fast
strangers strangers strangers.
an old man stumbled over the gutter
i leant over to help him
"Leave me alone", he grumbled
he wanted to be alone
i don't want to be alone anymore
faces bombarded me laughing sneering
reading my thoughts
i ran towards a lane way
crashing into a priest at the corner
looking up from the ground i screamed
"Father O'Brien. No! No! No!.
ice surged through my body
i choked on cold fear
"What ever's the matter my child?"
i screamed out, "Get away"
and ran off wildly,
through zooming cars,
knocking people over.
room, my room,
had to get to my room
i collapsed on my bed
Father O'Brien's voice penetrated my soul
wicked child,
you wicked, wicked child.

<u>Personal Diary</u>   15th March 1998

(recollection of 10th October 1997)

memories came back
not traces, not bits
huge chunks of burning memories.
foster parent's cruelty,
locked in tiny cupboards
starving for days,
being shuffled around like a thing,
never belonging,
never anywhere long enough to belong.
i longed to belong,
i prayed for help
NONE CAME!
NONE!
the agony of Father O'Brien abusing my body,
he'd force me to pray after he hurt me
he hurt me so many times
he told me to pray because i was wicked,
he told me the devil lived in me
my voices were the devil's voice.
Now Father O'Brien's voice kept screaming
i held my head
wicked child,
you wicked, wicked child.
i lay on my bed frozen with fear for days,
"Get your pills!"
"Get the Clozapine!"

i crawled across the floor
wicked, wicked child ha! ha! ha!
i'll make you pay for your wickedness.
tomorrow - when we're alone.
i gulped down a handful of pills,
the lights faded
my mind numbed
the room faded into darkness.

<u>Personal Diary</u>   <u>6th April 1998</u>

i'm back in my room
months have gone, how many?
a blur
too many days not crossed off the calendar
i must start again
i'm still alive, how? why?
trying new medication - RISPERIDONE
they treat me like an experiment
i'm a person you know!
BASTARDS!
i can't talk to people,
i can't socialise,
i know i'll never have friends.
i can't watch TV
they all laugh and have fun,
i can't join in
they never answer me when i talk.
i bought a potted house plant,

a weeping fig,
i need some company.
i wonder if plants like people
i wonder,
weeping fig do you like me?

<u>Personal Diary</u>   6th April 1998

The buses come and go,
flashes of memories come and go
ECT fades my memories
.....ELECTRO CONVULSIVE THERAPY.....
big words still frighten me.
flashes of light now and then,
all my people links are gone
Mrs Streng must have stolen them
she spies on me,
steals my things when i go for walks.
i walk in the park each day
i talk to birds and flowers
i have to talk to someone.
Dr Mazzner's secretary typed a letter for me, she said,
"This will get an apology from the Church",
i kissed the letter for luck
dropping it carefully in the post box
i'm feeling agitated waiting,
waiting, waiting.
i start crossing days of the calendar
again

i don't feel much pain anymore
sort of - just numb
too numb to even cry.

****

Cardinal Bell
The Church of Australia
GPO 666
Canberra ACT 2601

1st June 1998

Dear Katrina,

Regarding the letter sent from Dr. Mazzner's office concerning your claims of abuse by Father Obrien we can find no evidence that you were ever abused, sexually or in any other way, in the said Diocese. Therefore any claims you have against Father O'Brien and the Church will not be taken any further. They are clearly a fabrication of your imagination.

However, in keeping with the growing number of genuine abuse claims against the Church, which have been resolved in the claimants' favour we admit that it is possible you could have been abused. We apologise if this ever happened and offer you the enclosed cheque as a token of compensation. This compensation in no way constitutes an admission of guilt on the part of The Church.

This matter is now closed.

Cardinal Bell

****

Dear Dr Mazzner,   *2nd June 1998*

finally, this letter arrived from The Church yesterday morning.

as you can see the lying creeps deny everything but still offer compensation? for me, reading between the lying lines, this is a complete admission of guilt by The Church.

i don't care about the money offered but i now feel like a new person. a huge weight of false guilt for all these years has suddenly been lifted from me. it has just vanished, GONE!

I know i'm going to get better now, i'll see you next week to get some lighter medication.

wishes, katrina

Exaltation of The Neanderthal

Murray was a subhuman redneck,
well educated nonetheless
exalting the Australian Way
celebrating crass racism
wallowing in conservatism.
Deep in "the wide brown land"
words and lines carved in its dust
drift out to a fish-less, once blue ocean
staining a dying reef with shame.

2019 – Murray died
a wonderful poet nonetheless,
but not immortal.
2019 - National Neanderthals re-elected
Australians embrace and exalt
a "path well trodden",
the path to Extinction,
rejoicing with a perverse pleasure
mindlessly signing their children's death certificates
in black coal dust.

Who will say "Sorry" in 2050?
when the choking stench,
the stench of 7.5 billion corpses
escapes the once blue planet
to pollute the universe for eternity.

Layers

My psychiatrist is an expert
she specialises in two stories,
Pseudo logia Fantastica
Post Traumatic Stress Syndrome,
every week she analyses me layer on layer
she stresses I should write poetry.

I do my research and find astonishing things,
she herself is a pathological liar,
I ponder Epimendes paradox
he, a Cretan philosopher said,
"All Cretans are liars"
I write poetry layer on layer
building stories, great edifices about liars.
List #1:
Politicians
Bankers
Media Manipulators
Priests
Vacuum Cleaner Salesmen
Drug dealers
Whores.

Why am I seeing a shrink? - because;
List #2
I was abused
I was lied to
I was told I was the Village Idiot
I have too many post traumatic stresses to deal with
I was expelled from school.

I was expunged from the National Party - why?
List#3
lobbying for humane treatment of animals
advocating action against climate change

advocating the telling of truth
advocating not insulting their prospective voters
lobbying for affordable housing for all.

The shrink says I suffer from OCD,
I write too many lists, with corrections and Addenda.
these drift past me with possible answers,
layers and lists are multiplying
fictions about fictional fabrications.

Saskia Olde Wolbers an apparition
hypnotises with her fantastical landscapes.
Has she read Antonin Artaud?
his *"Theatre of Cruelty"* mesmerising,
her *"Theatre of Fictions"* deceiving!

Logic no longer exists,
an anachronistic aberration of the Enlightenment,
my shrink quotes Ducasse
I think it is time to stop seeing her?
analysis of lies and fictions
all becoming a convoluted web
a tragic web of deceptions.
Ducasse *'The Comte de Lautréamont'*
slips in-to and out-of a warped reality,
from very proper chaste prude
to depraved insane sadistic avatar.

I have shopping to do, my list is never finished;
List#4
2 tins sardines in oil
2 tins sardines in spring water
50 tins of anchovies
choc-chip-cream biscuits
200 mini bottles of tonic water
1 box of matches

(These to light a fire, a funeral pyre,
a bonfire under my sneaky, slippery, schizoid, shrink!)

Drink The Blood

The clones of the dominant order bow,
entering 2 x 2,
tendrils reach out grabbing at their superiority
like intractable vagrants loitering in alleys
dark, filthy laneways of disgust,
too insane to think
too stupid to lift the dark corners,
those filth filled attics of their minds
which blind them to reality.

Reality Remains!

The PAEDOPHILES enter 1 x 1
scourges of a disintegrating edifice of evil.
Drink the blood, eat the bread!
destroy young lives through fear,
behind the Mea culpa lattice foil,
Criss-cross – Criss-cross,
Drink the blood, eat the bread
disguised as the Corpus Christi.
Perform your celibate rituals with no consent,
pagan-like in lonely vestibules and niches.

I prayed to angels once,
they left me abandoned in the gutter garbage,
"You want it darker?" the Master asks,
"You want it blacker?"
the darkness is absolute,
symbols on the chill wind scream,
the black robed monsters
filled with uncontrollable desire
are sucked down into the vortex of hell,
No Confiteor,
No sacrament of Penance.

"Christ Broken – East Lismore" (Photo Robert Maddox-Harle)

Stockhausen's Attack

the music drew me out of the darkness
out of the dark labyrinthine tunnel,
mesmerising colours and notes surround me
engulfing me totally,
changing augmentation, diminution,
transformation, adaptation, substitution
threatened to explode my fragile mind,

con fuoco   with fire   con fuoco

gradually the softer intensities predominate
suddenly a staccato attack
attacked me
then fell to a legato articulation,

retardando   slower   retardando

soon the softer interval fields prevailed
gradually decaying into a force-field of no-thingness
then into absolute silence

silence   silence   silence

Farewell Lady Luna!

I suspected Lady Luna would be sad
But No!
laughter lifted the night sky,
the mysterious mistress of darkness
intoxicated with humour
sent forth mocking shrills
amused by the extreme stupidity,
the utter unworldly naivety
of the human imbeciles below her gaze.
But was her mirth a little premature?

"We'll mine the moon for aluminium!"
"We've trashed the earth, let's move on out?"
techno-evangelists, ruthless entrepreneurs
devoid of wisdom
devoid of any moral conscience
destroying that which they cannot perceive.

Lover's spirits uplifted by her pale silvery glow,
Lady Luna enchanting, enigmatic
inspiring artists and poets
regulating tides and flow of blood
the invisible essence of life itself.
The "dark side" holds arcane secrets,
secrets the imbeciles will never know
could never dream of in their haste to extinction.

And now on cold clear nights
when all below is deathly silent,
walking alone through remnant forest glades
I'll see the hideous shadows of excavators
sickly yellow-grey, trashing the moon

and hear faintly the despair,
the laughter changed to Lady Luna weeping.

Delayed Departure

I awoke from a death-like sleep
the sky was glowing alizarin – crimson - gold
slivers of sunlight dissolved the Morning Star
Lady Luna banished to The Underworld.
.

Today I will cross the Universe entire
transcending the constraints of space-time
(silly old Einstein)
travelling at the speed of thought
preparing for departure I suddenly froze
realisation of my planned day overwhelmed me.

Coffee and cake @ ten with a friend
lunch @ one with my publisher
cleaning the toilet @ three
get up – get going – get breakfast
grape juice – gluten free toast – ground coffee
check email – check messages – check my look
get going do it! – get going do it!

Creamy croissant – Cappuccino coffee – chatter chatter
gotta go – gotta go – gotta go
no parking spots
damn – damn - damn
park on the outskirts and walk
plod crunch – plod crunch – plod crunch
LGBTQ café – BLT+chilli – VF,GF,DF mud cake
sign the book contract – Culture In Synchrony With Dust
establish time lines
credits – contributors - collaborators
plod crunch – plod crunch – plod crunch
speeding home – cruising along – Pink Floyd blasting.

Bucket and broom – bottle of bleach – bristle brush
swish – swirl – squeegee – sanitise
collapse on the lounge exhausted.

Maybe I will transcend the Universe tomorrow?

Sonnet For The Earth

Do leaves that fall on cold and windy days
Ever think they are destined for an early death?
Yes, they know they're passing through a phase
As Autumn changes into Winter's frozen breath.

Both young and old must respect this yearly cycle
Even if their inventions and shelters intervene,
No good calling nature an annoying trifle
When all that is and has been can be seen.

Tread lightly on this green earth so delicate
No place for careless trash and hasty burn,
Every vile pollution and chemical distillate
Poisons little insects which ever way they turn.

Careless humans transcend your old foolish ways
And sing sweetly for the remainder of your days.

The Blazing Furnace

The void of nature's womb is flowering
separation – coagulation - transubstantiation
impossibility has no meaning in the blazing furnace,
years of toil attending the fire
years of misunderstanding fall away,
salt – mercury - sulphur
the foundations of The Stone
align in dynamic equilibrium,
settling happily in the ethereal vessel.

The silicone Messiah is knocking
pulsing down society's mind
tempting the slickest-stained-clones
bolstering the gallows of capitalism
tensioning the fractured face of stress.
Young generations grow syntactically sharp
believing the great false prophets
dripping with aborted foetuses of greed,
their lies glide past the wise
and dissolve into the blackness of eternity.

The vessel is still,
the perfect marriage consummated,
all is calm in the dull orange reduction.

The womb-like furnace has reached parturition
the blazing reducing to a glow of universal knowing,
dancing on the landscape of hope
avoiding the tangled bird netting of delusion,
soaring outwards
like invisible ripples on the pond
the fluid flowing sea of existence,
The Stone is ready!

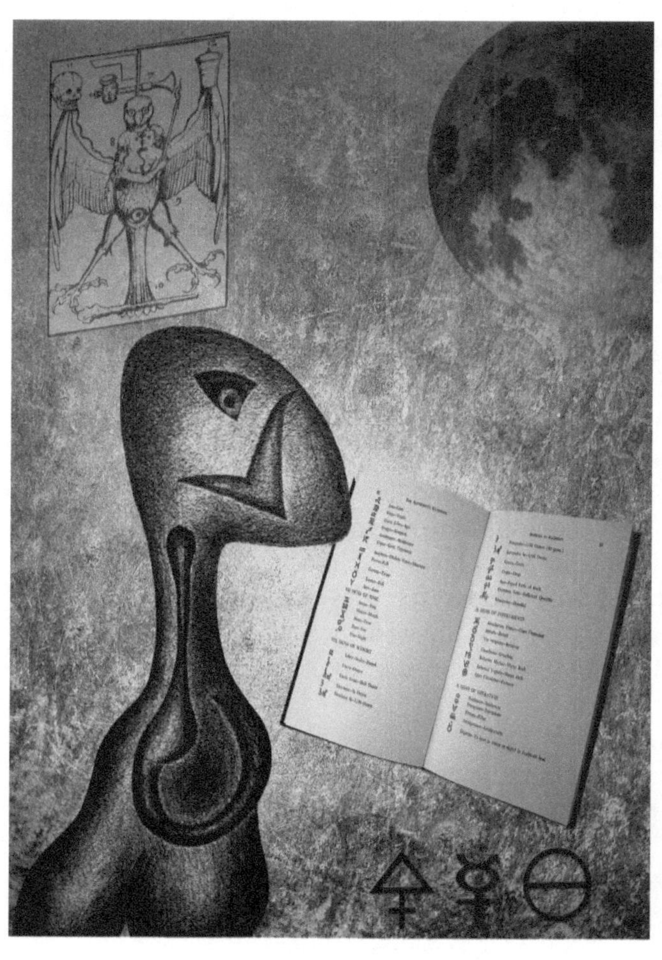

Preparation for the Great Work (Original artwork Robert Maddox-Harle)

Postmodern Funeral Lecture

Part 1 Tomorrow's Lecture Prep.
The interpretation must include the intention
exposing the second-hand reflective narrative
they think we do not understand
lines which are difficult to be forgiven
no longer safe with the quality of ignorance
a new world pulling aside obscure veils
they are emancipating words considered authorless.

Part 2
Ding-dong! Ding-dong! Ding-dong!
What is it?
Parcel for you!
Thanks!
Ah - my book on postmodern mental masturbation,
ebay number 2341234a23.
This book an authorless tome by Jacques De-reader
Eight hundred and eighty eight pages
an explication of the theory of postmodern nihilism.
Conclusion: Everything amounts to nothing.

Part 3 Back to the Prep.
"Postmodern theory is pure mental masturbation
BUT without the possibility of ever achieving orgasm."
I anticipate the response:
"Depends how you define orgasm."
My rejoinder:
"If you have to define orgasm you'll never have one!"
The de-struction of postmodernism is nigh.
Let us now talk about psychoanalytical theory,
this is postmodernism's inbred idiot cousin.
Talking about an umbrella
or dreaming of carrots must mean,

Penis Envy!
It might actually be raining tomorrow?

Part 4 Reflection
The most important consideration tomorrow is,
apart from rain
What sort of pie will I get for lunch?
Plain meat, chilli curry, mushroom-cheese mornay?
I just cannot decide,
oh the obscurantinism
oh the post-structural confusion
Why?
The author of the pies is unknown,
the signifier is lying!
I am trapped in an mindless void of nihilistic nothingness!

The Printery

The door protests angrily at its rusted hinges
shifting gloom seduces my eyes,
cautiously I enter the abandoned printery
closed since the War – dusty and dirty
printing presses, ink vats, racks of assembled Type
like little dead soldiers
– waiting for commands:
racks of discoloured paper in their shuttles
– waiting:
cracked and peeling paint hangs motionless
faded metal operating instructions balance precariously
bare electric globes sticky with spider's silk
- waiting to be energised:
machines, tools, motors in suspended animation
- waiting:

Treading carefully I climb a steel ladder with rusted rungs
the mezzanine floor's rusted checker-plate steel groans,
I step softly holding my breath
a red storeroom-like door arouses my curiosity
deathly silence rings my ears,
nudging the door to open – creak – creak,
pallid light descends from a yellowed skylight,
the room obviously a foreman's office
dust coat neatly folded on the chair
cap and once-white-gloves neatly sit on the timber desk,
intrepidly I enter - adrenalin pumping
brushing against a large metal switch
the power of a tornado slams me to the floor
rolling over I gasp for air
I lay wondering if I am going to die
the electric shock merciless.

The light in the office glaring at me
I hear machinery starting
click, clunk – click, clunk – click, clunk
the printing press running up to speed,
I stagger to my feet
looking down I see the bare globes glowing,
the main press drags in paper
sheets of print emerge like clockwork
click, print, slide, stack - click, print, slide, stack.

Frightened I descend the rusted ladder
the press is furiously printing
mesmerised I stand waiting for the run to finish,
fifty pages have emerged ink stains on the edges.
"The Final Works of the Comte de Lautréamont",
 impossible - Isidore Ducasse died at twenty four
many, many years ago
a mysterious literary genius,
all extant works published and acknowledged?

Sitting on the filthy bench I read,
possessed I read faster and faster
indeed – must be his last lost literary work,
numb with disbelief I wobbled to the door
the manuscript safely stashed in my bag,
slamming the old front door – thud,
I head for home shivering and shaking.

"The Printery" (Still from the Quay Bros. film "Street of Crocodiles" 1986)

Days Like This

Remember the list
Yes! Yes!
eggs, milk, toilet paper, bleach
the flowering geranium – brilliant red
beckons me, "Go forth,"
Call +61 0427 000666
"Sing a song of sixpence,
A pocket full of rye."
This means add bread to the list,
eggs, milk, toilet paper, bleach, bread.
Got it!

Screaming through the traffic
mercilessly peddling my bicycle faster,
harder - faster,
I duck and weave
curse and swear,
the glowing shop looms closer.

Crash, my Smartphone falls to the ground,
deep black bitumen wounds
the Contacts spill across the blackness
how can I save these noble souls?
"Sweep them into a reusable plastic bag"
"I knew this you idiot!"
Call +61 0427 000666
"Why? Why should I?"

Car horns blast me into the gutter
"Clean gutters = Clean rivers"
the sign insults and assaults my senses,
sirens scream from all directions
I've lost my list,

smashed my phone,
left my money at home,
broken my bike,
"Then carry it home you idiot!"
Call +61 0427 000666
Some days are like this.

Howling Dogs

The mysteries of the dispossessed
expose layers of our inner existence
where magic hides inside the heart,
where the Media – the ultimate insidious evil
(almost more evil than the Church)
tells us what to think
tells us what to believe
who to hate - who to love - who to kill
the subtle Pavlovian programming hidden,
secretly, silently behind screaming TV screens,
behind silent typeset tabloids
behind seductive ads in glossy zines,
there the Pavlovian dogs howl.

Ayn Rand, too many years ago exposed the plot
nobody bothered to listen,
perhaps the dumbing down had started then
dogs howling at an empty moon.

The magic in our hearts, ever present
occulted by a smoke screen of deception,
smoke screens of sensationalism
blatant manipulative lies
weighed down by the media's atrocities
can no longer fly - light and free
no longer dream of halcyon days
or days (and nights) of wine and roses.

Greed has reached its zenith of glory
Supreme Greed Rules!
greed has encased our hearts
the always present magic trapped
like a Pavlovian dog in its cage with bars invisible

aching for an escape
to share the beauty of nature,
the miracles of existence
to be our unique selves once more
not mindless pawns of the maggot-like media moguls.

The Way

Out of the *black chaotic cloud* of being,
the alchemical *prima materia*
emerges perfect order,
equilibrium and calmness defy Chaos.
Masters of The Tea Ceremony sit serenely,
within a silence of perfection
seemingly in defiance of the *massa confusa,*
but the composure will soon collapse.

Like the conjuror's stage set
the background sea-of-light is illusive
each photon mirrored by a mirror photon,
and – like the conjuror's set of mirror trickery
deceives the unwary.

Allegories of alchemy show the way,
spiritual traditions point to the way,
ancient philosophies hint at the way,
The Tao is The Way!
Screaming in perfect silence.

The Club of the Laid Off

inducted into The Club,
the *"Club of the Laid Off"*
I noticed names graffitied carelessly,
smeared over deathly grey concrete walls
Kafka, Barta, Sartre
Camus, Quay Bros., Nietzsche
et al. et al. et al.

landing at the dusty bar
like a vulture over a carcass,
i ordered – absinthe, double
straight with ice
"God is Dead"
Yes! What else can you tell me?
"Life is Absurd"
Yes! What else can you tell me?
"The author is dead"
Oh really! Who wrote this poem?

how wonderful? how cathartic?
no more paternal expectations
no more foul excrement from above,
Kafka new this well,
read *"Letter to my Father"* from Franz"!

another absinthe, more ice
Where is the theatre of the Absurd?
"Down that endless corridor."
Is Artaud in residence?
"Like a shadow he comes and goes!"
Yes! Like a Philip Glass tonal derangement
in a straightjacket of fiery embers,
Powaqqatsi – Powaqqatsi – Powaqqatsi.

how empowering this absurdity?
no longer reason rules,
not to be dragged through the morgue of reality,
Absurd, God-less Reality Reigns Supreme,

Wittgenstein tried to maintain non-absurdity
become shopkeepers you brain dead sheep
"What type of shop?"
Too late, already trapped
deep in the mire of *"larval confusion"*.

The Club rejects many applications,
Derrida, Barthes, Kristeva, Foucault
all turned away mercilessly,
too much reason ….. the reason.
Einstein's ghost waits patiently to enter,
acceptance or rejection?,
to roam the labyrinths of darkness.

Karlheinz Stockhausen prowling
always present but never seen
shrieks and shrills and clangs in the dark corridors,
endless passages leading nowhere
endless repeats, repeats, repeats, repeats.

NB: "The Club of the Laid Off" (1989) is a short 25 minute stop-frame animation
movie masterpiece by Czech filmmaker Jiri Barta.

"The Club" (Original photo and artwork Robert Maddox-Harle)

Silent Shadows

In her eerie light
between clouds obscuring
the moon sheds her beauty.
Dancing across the trees
shadows play a pantomime of intrigue.

The intrigue grows loud
shrieking – shrieking - growing louder
the forest, deathly still reverberates,
shriek – boom – shriek – boom,
ghostly figures filter through trees
pulsing slowly to the tune of terror.

Deep low moaning echoes
overwhelm the shrieking shadows,
moan – murmur – moan
moaning – moaning –whining loudly,
falling thumps agitate the forest floor,
blackened leaves rustle – crunching down
crunching under invisible feet,
thud – thud – thud
the thudding - rustling - crunching
growing louder – harder – louder,
brighter - pulsing brighter - glowing brighter

Shush!
Shush!
softening – slowing – silence
Silence – silence – silence.

Kittens Chasing Leaves

The ultimate abstract symbolic creation,
language - little marks on a page
deceptively simple representations
invoking a grammar to beat on a stage
blowing across our frontal lobes
to make windborne patterns,
are these a gang of evil spirits
aesthetic magico artworks
tricking us into a fall from direct experience.

A naked artist emerges from the jungle,
Congo painted many artworks
colourful, intentional, balanced, intense
he had not heard of Pollock or Warhol
did not know of Warhol's Marilyn Monroe
did not know it would sell for $195,000,000,
Art (with a capital A) reinforces elitist, ideological agendas
the artist, other than Name, irrelevant
an illusory commodity marketed as cultural bullion,
wonder how much Congo's paintings sell for?

Kittens playing with shadows
sweet melodious birds singing
dolphins surfing cresting waves
cockroaches cleaning the detritus of humanity
all fulfilling their destinies.
insane humans once worshipped a God
a mythological invisible absentee god
now the worship has changed to lip service
the dollar has supplanted god
becoming the supreme deification of Greed.

Congo unaware of the folly of humans

dolphins unaware
birds and cockroaches unaware
children in their innocent world unaware,
their world blessed with non-functional embellishment
reinforcing positive emotional significance,
and the kitten chases dancing leaves
stirred by a carefree breeze.

In The Forest

the sinister night above pushed down,
Lady Luna's eerie light teased me
breaking through the careless clouds
light enough to find the trembling track.

the forest a welcoming friend by day
turned menacing towards the witching hour.
soon the dark swallowed my shaky steps
Crunch - Crunch - Trudge - Trudge
freshly fallen leaves crunched upwards,
night birds screeching tore the blackness apart
suddenly - mercilessly,
then deathly silence
deathly quite
deathly stillness.

a faint glimmer glistened
reflecting in the tiny stream below,
loose pebbles threatened my walking
Carefully - Carefully
Crash - I hit the ground
cascading downwards through the bushes
sliding on slippery stones
gouged by sharp twigs.
the glimmer grew brighter
Brighter - Brighter.
I lay shaken
gasping by the gurgling stream,
the glimmer sharpened slowly
forming a pulsing figure.

"WHAT ARE YOU DOING HERE?" I stammered
"I told you brother from my death bed,

I would give you a sign!"
I lay on the cold earth stuttering,
"Yes, but it's been fifteen years!"
"This mysterious forest is a portal,
a space-time anomaly."
"Sad you had to depart so soon,
your girls are fine,
your grandchildren are fine."

His presence shifted in its floating
"What is the 'Other Side' like?"
"Strange and hard to traverse -
all to do with harmonic resonance!" he exclaimed
"Many Dimensions!
"Takes much energy to come through,
cannot stay any longer."

His ghostly figure faded
as the glimmer dissipated.
the hard ground pushed upwards,
transfixed -sobbing
I tried to stand.
a large owl shrieked
circling above me,
huge oval eyes, penetrating
watched me stumbling,
staggering my way out of the forest.

"In the Forest" (photo Robert Maddox-Harle)

A Story To Tell

Within the deposits of their existence
they search frantically for answers
perhaps to replace insecure identities,
many are deeply involved with injustices
that haunt and hurt,
these identities shaped by lies and deception
seek therapy to flow with a gentle cadence.

Just when I was confident of tenure
the spectre of Mario Bellatin surged in,
he kept his testicles in a box
became a pseudo Sufi
wrote numerous non non-autobiographies,
I wondered if his "Large Glass" was

half full

or

half empty

but

then I realised in an epiphany
I-did-not-care-less,
Bellatin is whirling in circles,
I have a story to tell!

Yes gentle cadence floats easily
rising, falling with the autumn breeze
flowing harmoniously with the Tao,
I ponder the plight of Sisyphus
poor fool locked in an endless loop

a loop of his own making (Zeus notwithstanding)
condemned to dance in the dark firmament
no chance of finding a light switch.

Bellatin keeps moving in and out of my psyche,
why does his transvestite hairdresser
(who only wears synthetic wigs)
create a mortuary for young men?
they come to die together
their disease unknown,
possibly AIDS or Covid I ponder,
Is Bellatin a Sufi seer
a prophet tearing the future apart?

Sisyphus, Bellatin and Saskia Olde Wolbers
move easily between dream and reality
signposts blur as we cascade downwards
dragged onwards into dark unknowns
regions where gravity is suspended,
where time flows forwards and backwards
where truth and fiction merge unnoticed.

I have a story to tell,
it will have to wait till then
I've been possessed again by another spectre
that of the enigmatic Sophie La Rosière!

"Power" (Original photo Carl Heydon)

Lost In Dimension 7

the austerity of the black hole
jolted me out of my apathetic slumber,
with the creation of dynamic information
it pushes the credibility of truth.

for those who lock themselves into answers
having a sensitive dependence on dogma
new qualities are offered with Hopf bifurcations.

I sat tensely with a spell over my mind,
finding parts of the harmonic proofs
the music began to decay
and tore mercilessly into the water.

defined by an idea of deconstruction
I pondered,
was this a coincidence with non-local effects
which was self-similar scale-invariant
and emitting a sensuous soft red haze?

pulsating with the reflection of mangroves in her eyes
the warm air caressed my shouting,
vacuous messages devoid of substance
taunted this ethereal gypsy.

injustices of the soul
echo, "Lament to a Silent Place",
always the enigmatic imagery abounds.

my hand tightened around the sky
in the unknown recesses of dimension seven
as the isolated reaches of silence opened.

Cyborg in Paradise

I came to paradise as human
faltering, staggering with each step
a chance of DNA the fault
part coding gone awry.

then scans and images
needles and knives
meds and tubes and monitors
drugs and drips.

five hours in the land of blackness
I emerged as Cyborg
titanium, polyethylene and super-glue,
I Cyborg transformed
resurrected from my own artwork
taller, straighter, younger
ready to fly to the moon.

tall buildings
sky-scrapers of obscenity
kept me grounded
each one vying for grid Position One
each greedily blocking the others' view
each demanding an artificial life
devoid of the nurture of nature
I Cyborg still grounded
cannot leap these tall buildings.

Now Selling!
everything in this greedy paradise is
Now Selling!
the price is far too high
I Cyborg leave The Strip

retreating to a place of grass and trees
where birds and lizards rule
far from The Strip
where lights and traffic rule,
where sirens rip the days and nights apart.

The Mysterious Sophie La Rosière

Dressed in a shining robe of the deepest black
Sophie mixed the black encaustic wax,
painting after painting she imprisoned
hiding them, but not destroying.

Why the door paintings?
leaving her early still lifes untouched,
leaving Florence's paintings untouched.
The door paintings, erotic masterpieces,
a record of their tumultuous love affair.
Sophie's despair at the end of the affair,
her devastation when Florence left
too much to see each day
a graphic reminder of overwhelming lust and love,
the final act of entombing with encaustic
a melancholic suicide.
Was the enigmatic Sophie exhausted?
Had she lost her will to create?
To live?

A hundred years since the encaustic erasure
x-rays, planning, preparation, cleaning, exposure,
masters of alchemical transformation revealed the truth,
exposing works of exquisite erotic beauty,
we are left wondering
would Sophie be happy with this?
Did she know or hope this might happen
on that black Parisian night
when the encaustic wax flowed with her tears?

Important Dates:

1867 Sophie La Rosière (nee Basset) born at Nogent-sur-Marne
1905 Sophie inherits family home joins Paris art scene
1907 Sophie develops intimate relationship with Florence
1908 Florence moves in with Sophie (1908 – 1918)
1918 Florence leaves for Paris and all trace of her vanishes
1947 Sophie moves to Maison de artistes, brings with her " a set
of black artworks painted on dismantled furniture", some paintings
made on door panels, she refused to be separated from them.
1948 Sophie dies.

Reference:
The Sophie La Rosière Project by Iris Häussler
2018 Art Gallery of York University, Toronto
ISBN: 978-0-921972-73-0

Allegro Vivace

adventures come and go
days fly by in a mesmerising hurtle,
nail it down
slow it down
the race to death is too hectic.

seems like yesterday
fixing dad's vintage Victor mower,
sixty five years have slipped by
days crossed off the calendar
a calendar of unknown finitude,
a pile of days dissolved like morning mist,
constant battles against unnecessary angst
have etched their marks too deep.

family ties both East and West
the tyranny of distance hard
but still we made the effort,
now all but two are gone
one East and one out distant West,
different oceans different shores apart.

Dvorak dissolves my largo introspection
throwing me to the floor in rapture,
Adagio - Allegro Molto
Largo
Molto vivace
Allegro
"New World' in E Minor roars,
roaring, dipping, diving
a cascading avalanche of orchestral bliss
testing the glass of old windows,
Moderato

Tempo Di Valse
Scherzo
Larghetto
"Finale" - Allegro Vivace,
and now I am young again.

The Mannequin

Crimson nightmares survive
the angels block injury from flying indigo glass
sharp shards exploding,
above this tension a mannequin cuts loose
bursting through her milky-white repressions,
remorselessly she senses the stimulus
naturally – carefully - intensely
she seduces the voyeur,
a marble-grey-white seductress
she bulges out of her skimpy lingerie
selling promises that fall short,
far short of the drunk's late night desires
he stares longingly into the boutique window.

The nightmares become etchings
permanently engraved Kafka-like
deep into the mannequin's belly,
alabaster complexion with blue-black tattoos,
the drunk curses her ashen-grey smirk
then staggers towards the Underground.

No lurking voyeurs in sight
she takes a coffee break
slinking snake-like out of her glass niche.

Manifestos cling to the warm pink surfaces
the extravagant lingerie boutique sells promises of lust,
a naive nun, a genius and two sorry ghosts
marvel at the mannequin,
now her black satin dress partly hides the lingerie,
the nun shuffles uneasily in her habit
perhaps a transvestite in dull brown-black drag,
rosary hanging limply between false breasts

trolling for more dark doorway satisfaction
wondering if the mannequin's lingerie will fit
partially to cover her pumped and pierced genitals.

The genius takes notes,
recording data for future analysis,
calculating probabilities of Quantum desire
unaware of the ghost's fleeting presence.

The ghosts hurry towards the Underground
fearful the time eating the Town Clock
will expose their hidden desires,
stupidly they slam into a feral artist's painting
sending his easel and paints sideways,
the scarlet red smears the pavement
creating a psychoanalyst's Rorschach deception.

The mannequin smiles smugly
secure behind her glass cage
at one with its seductive secrets.

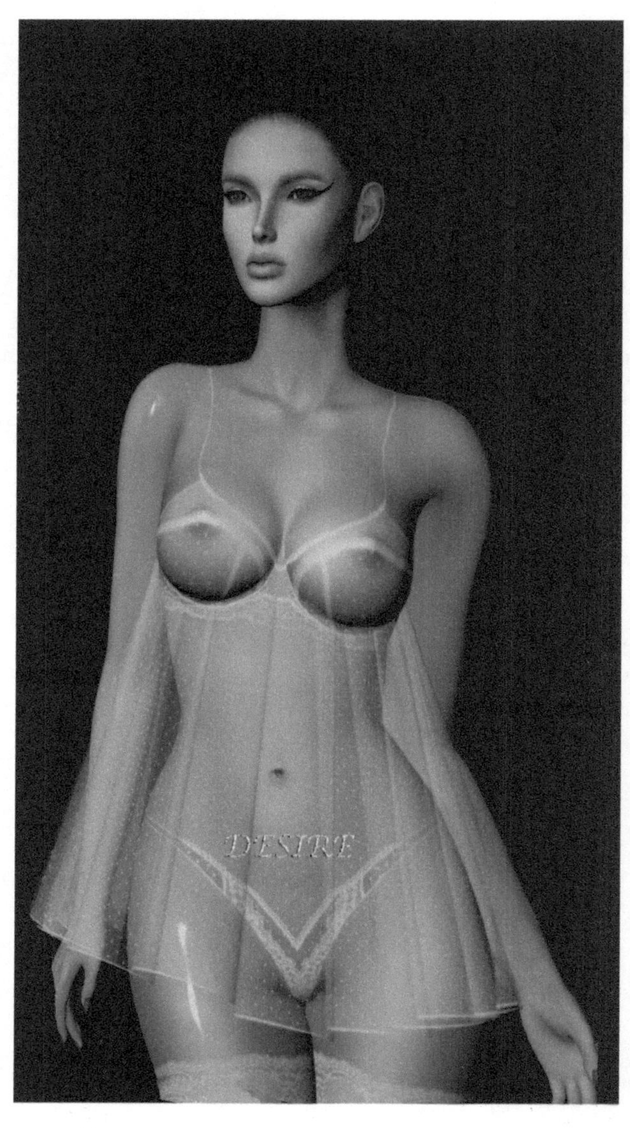

"The Mannequin" (Secondlife photo by Robert Maddox-Harle)

Quantum Vagrancy

The illusory nature of inexorable change,
with symmetry building ability,
has reached a temporal facet of its existence,
spontaneous emergence of fractal geometry
self-similar and scale-invariant collapses,
creation of oppressive deconstruction evolution
questions the maturity of quantum vagrancy.

The shopper is deeply entangled,
trapped between the shopping-list-lines:
500 grams pumpkin
one dozen eggs
two litres of white vinegar
ten packets jelly beans
100 grams Darjeeling tea
one packet split, black, French lentils.

The dawn of a background sea of light
looming across distorted horizons
far into the aminergic-cholinergic system
has caused a higher dimensional phase space,
a place to hang your hat
a place to call home
a place where no one can intrude.
Do not forget to put rum in the fruit cake!

Connected everywhere and nowhere brings confusion,
spinning through the sixth dimension
travelling fast, travelling alone
the great perturbations of Brahman's breath
crash the infallible systems of control,
and the illusory effects of the oldest symbols,
in cyclic return

have become strange attractors.

Grandma suggested salt is a good stain remover
rugs, shirt fronts, socks,
all will respond to the treatment,
slightly dampened, left for five minutes.

The alchemical treatise De Lapide Philisophico
heralds the dawn of archetypes,
the symbols of unbroken wholeness.

And Grandma agrees!

Requiem for "The Old Dart"

In days of old the serfs were sold
and England's Kings and Queens were bold,
But now the writing's on the wall
from Sydney Cove to Downing Street and all.

The Republican's flag is biting deep
behind dosed doors the lonely royalists weep,
a hope to fly the Jack from yards of old
that now are paved with guiltless Green and Gold.

And where's the colours Black – Yellow – Red
Indigenous culture shattered - nearly dead,
The sacred land is being torn apart
it's time to listen and repair her crippled heart.

For God and Commonwealth we bled
now commonwealth and god are dead,
And where the hell's this wealth so common
in vaults beneath a throne bequeathed by flogg'n.

So - computer chips spew out the news
from satellites in front row pews,
But still the stallions drag the carriage
of last century's most celebrated marriage.

But remember when the colony becomes oppressive!

There'll always be an England
A land of cold and pain,
Of superiority, pomp and circumstance
And rain and rain and rain.

Cast Shadows

The abandoned building beckons
a bleak bridge to the past,
paint flakes the wall
falling like downcast eyes,
an eerie dull light seeps insipidly
from a crescent moon,
a flickering dull-bright from
the cracks beneath the antique doors.

Damp musty scents waft over me
the presence of coal gas menacing,
somewhere a clock ticks loudly
reinforcing the curse of mortality,
Plath's ghost sighs deeply
trying to recite *Sheep In Fog,*
impossible this side of the bleak bridge.

The one armed cook smirking
stirs the blood filled stew
and the broken stove creaks,
dinner for the Laid Off
half warm - soon.
the boy's clock chimes his return
his broken lamp lifeless
casting shadows on nothing!

(Inspired by "The Club of the Laid Off" (1989) is a short 25 minute stop-frame animation
movie masterpiece by Czech filmmaker Jiri Barta.

Glass Progressions

attenuate >>>> attenuate >>>> attenuate
silence …. loud …. silence
onward
louder >>>> louder >>>> louder
fortissimo
shrill-stop < > shrill-stop < > shrill-stop
densely packed hard sonorities
accelerando >>>> accelerando >>>> accelerando
faster
unstoppable linear progressions
unstoppable …. unstoppable
accelerandro >>>> accelerando >>>> accelerando
imminent climax < > denial …. imminent climax < > denial
gradually slowing
adagio >>>> adagio >>>> adagio
hypnotic
hypnotic-deep …. hypnotic-deep …. hypnotic-deep
trance
trance-murmur …. trance-murmur …. trance-murmur
hush …. hush …. hush
euphoria …. flowing …. euphoria
onward …. onward …. onward

Inspired by: "Glassworks" - Philip Glass 1982

**Other books written, edited or co-edited by Robert Maddox-Harle
(aka Rob Harle)**

***Searching For The Sublime: Poems from Australia &
India*** (ed. Jaydeep Sarangi & Rob Harle) Cyberwit, India.
(2016)

Homeward Bound: Poems from Australia & India (ed.
Jaydeep Sarangi & Rob Harle) Cyberwit, India. (2015)

The Land: Poems from Australia & India (ed. Jaydeep
Sarangi & Rob Harle) Cyberwit, India. (2015)

PCK Prem Echoing Time and Civilisations (ed. Harle,
Sharma & Sharma) Authorspress, India. (2015)

Indo-Australian Anthology of Short Fiction (ed. Harle,
Sharma & Sharma) Authorspress, India. (2014)

Voices Across Generations: Poetry Past & Present (ed.
Rob Harle) Authorspress, India. (2014)

***Voices Across The Ocean: Poems from Australia &
India*** (ed. Rob Harle & Jaydeep Sarangi) Cyberwit, India.
(2014)

Indo-Australian Anthology of Contemporary Poetry
(ed. Sharma, Harle & Sharma) Authorspress, India. (2013)

Building Bridges: Poems from Australia & India (ed.
Rob Harle) Cyberwit, India. (2013)

The Clock by Diane Hosking (ed. Rob Harle) Spinning Spider Publications, Australia. (2004)

Scratches & Deeper Wounds Poetry by Rob Harle Spinning Spider Publications, Australia. (1996)

Mechanisms Of Desire Poetry by Rob Harle Spinning Spider Publications, Australia. (2012)

Winds of Infinity Poetry by Rob Harle Cyberwit, India. (2016)